How to Use This ~~Book~~

A Variety of Presentations

1. Make overhead transparencies of the lessons. Present e~~ach~~ the entire class. Write answers and make corrections using an erasable marker.

   As the class becomes more familiar with *Daily Word Problems*, have students mark their answers first and then check them against correct responses marked on the transparency.

2. Reproduce the problems for individuals or partners to work on independently. Check answers as a group, using an overhead transparency to model the solutions' strategies. (Use these pages as independent practice only after much group experience with the lessons.)

3. Occasionally you may want to reproduce problems as a test to see how individuals are progressing in their acquisition of skills.

Important Considerations

1. Allow students to use whatever tools they need to solve problems. Some students will choose to use manipulatives, while others will want to make drawings.

2. It is important that students share their solutions. Modeling a variety of problem-solving techniques makes students aware that there are different paths to the correct answer. Don't scrimp on the amount of time allowed for discussing how solutions were reached.

3. Teach students to follow problem-solving strategies:
   - Read the problem carefully more than one time. Think about it as you read.
   - Mark the important information in the problem.
       What question does the problem ask?
       What words will help you know how to solve the problem (*in all*, *left*, *how many more*, etc.)?
       What facts will help you answer the question? (Cross out facts that are NOT needed.)
   - Think about what you need to do to solve the problem (add, subtract, multiply, or divide).
   - Solve the problem. Does your answer make sense?
   - Check your answer.

Matrix Logic Puzzles

The Friday problems for weeks 18, 32, and 34 are matrix logic puzzles. Here are some guidelines for helping students solve this type of logic puzzle:

   - Read all the clues. Find clues that give a definite *Yes* or *No*. (For example: John plays the clarinet. Sally does not play the flute.) Mark boxes with **X** (for no) or **Yes**.
   - When you mark a box **Yes**, mark Xs in all the other boxes in that row and in the column above and below the **X**.
   - Find clues that give information, but not enough to tell you how to mark the boxes. Make notes in the boxes for later use.
   - Go over each clue again. Look for clues that fit together to give enough information to make a box **Yes** or **No**.

Scope and Sequence—Grade 4

Week	1	2	3	4	5	6	7	8	9	10	11	12	13	14	15	16	17	18	19	20	21	22	23	24	25	26	27	28	29	30	31	32	33	34	35	36
Addition & Subtraction Facts	•								•																											
Addition & Subtraction, with and without Regrouping		•	•	•	•	•	•	•	•	•	•	•		•	•	•	•			•	•		•		•	•	•	•	•	•	•		•	•	•	•
Multiplication & Division Facts			•	•					•	•				•																	•	•				
Multiplication, without Regrouping														•	•					•	•		•		•	•	•					•		•	•	
Multiplication, with Regrouping	•			•		•	•				•	•						•			•		•		•	•			•	•	•		•	•		
Division, w/o Remainder	•		•					•					•					•										•			•					
Division, with Remainder											•	•									•				•										•	
Computation with Fractions	•			•		•				•			•			•						•	•		•			•								
Computation with Decimals, Percent																			•				•	•		•			•	•	•				•	•
Estimation					•						•				•				•					•												
Money	•		•	•		•	•	•	•	•	•	•	•					•				•	•									•	•	•		
Linear Measurement		•				•									•	•	•						•	•	•	•	•				•	•				
Weight and Capacity		•			•					•				•	•						•										•		•			•
Time		•			•	•	•	•	•			•	•		•		•		•	•					•				•	•	•			•	•	
Temperature					•														•									•								
Interpreting Graphs																											•									
Interpreting Data		•	•			•				•				•					•	•	•			•				•	•	•	•		•		•	•
Patterns						•			•	•														•			•						•			•
Logic Problems												•														•						•		•		•

Daily Word Problems

Monday-Week 1

School Supplies

Did you ever stop to think about how important math is when buying school supplies? Here is an example. Dan wants to have 2 pencils for every week of school. If there are 36 weeks of school, how many pencils will he need?

Name:

Work Space:

- 2 pencil / week
?   36 week

2 × 36

$$\begin{array}{r} 36 \\ \times 2 \\ \hline 72 \end{array}$$

Answer:

_____72_____ pencils

Daily Word Problems

Tuesday-Week 1

School Supplies

Dan uses 5 sheets of lined paper each day at school. He has 120 sheets of paper left over from last year. How many days will this paper last?

Name:

Work Space:

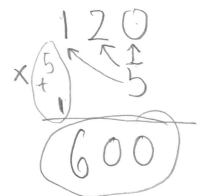

5 × 120

Answer:

_____600_____ days

Daily Word Problems

Wednesday-Week 1

School Supplies

Dan bought 1 glue stick for 56¢ and 2 pencils for 12¢ each. How much change should he get back from 1 dollar?

Name:

Work Space:

Answer:

$ _____

Daily Word Problems

Thursday-Week 1

School Supplies

Dan bought 10 computer disks. Each disk cost 98¢. How much did the computer disks cost in all?

Name:

Work Space:

98¢ X 10 = $9.80

Answer:

$9.80

Name: _____

School Supplies

Dan saw this ad in the newspaper for school supplies.

School Supplies

Backpack, $9.00

Markers, $2.25

Pencil bag, $1.75

Binder, $4.00

Colored pencils, $2.10

Pocket dictionary, $3.90

• How much will it cost to buy all of these school supplies?

_____

Daily Word Problems

Monday-Week 2

Seeds

Ms. Holloway's class wanted to find out how long it would take for a bean seed to begin to grow. First they placed seeds in jars that were lined with a moist paper towel. Draw a seed that is between $2\frac{1}{2}$ and 3 centimeters above the bottom of the jar.

Name:

Work Space:

5 cm ———
4 cm ———
3 cm ———
2 cm ———
1 cm ———
0 cm ———

Daily Word Problems

Tuesday-Week 2

Seeds

To keep the seeds moist, the students added $2\frac{1}{2}$ centiliters of water to the jars each school day. How many centiliters of water were added each week?

Name:

Work Space:

Answer:

_____ centiliters

Daily Word Problems
Wednesday-Week 2

Seeds

The seeds were put into jars on September 3rd. The first seed started to grow on September 7th. The last seed started to grow on September 10th. How long did it take for the first seed and the last seed to start to grow? How much longer did it take for the last seed to start to grow than the first seed?

Name:

Work Space:

Answer:

_____ days for the first seed

_____ days for the last seed

_____ days longer

Daily Word Problems
Thursday-Week 2

Seeds

Two weeks after all the seeds had started to grow, the class measured the length of the new growth. The length of the first plant's new growth was 106 millimeters. The length of the last plant's new growth was 57 millimeters. How much longer was the first plant's new growth?

Name:

Work Space:

Answer:

_____ millimeters longer

Name:

Seeds

The class made this chart to show the number of days it took for each seed to start to grow.

When the Seeds Started to Grow

	Seed A	Seed B	Seed C	Seed D	Seed E	Seed F
Number of Days	4	4	7	5	6	4

Use the chart to answer the following questions.

• Which seed or seeds took the most time to start growing?

_____

• Which seed or seeds took the least time to start growing?

_____

• • •

Seed A started to grow on day 4 and then grew 20 centimeters a day.
Seed C started to grow on day 7 and then grew 25 centimeters a day.

• Which plant was the first to reach 100 centimeters long?

_____

Daily Word Problems

Monday—Week 3

Student Council

Gail is a member of the student council. There are 30 student council members. If there are 2 members from each classroom, how many classrooms are there?

Name:

Work Space:

Answer:

_____ classrooms

Daily Word Problems

Tuesday—Week 3

Student Council

Members of the student council voted to have an all-day Read-A-Thon. The vote was 19 to 8. There are 30 members, so how many members did **not** vote?

Name:

Work Space:

Answer:

_____ members did not vote

Daily Word Problems

Wednesday-Week 3

Name:

Work Space:

Gail and Toby ran for student council president. A total of 405 students voted. Gail got 247 votes. How many students voted for Toby? Who won the election?

Answer:

_____ students voted for Toby

_____ won the election

Daily Word Problems

Thursday-Week 3

Name:

Work Space:

The student council held a fundraiser. They sold candy bars for $1.00 each, making a profit of 50¢ on each bar. The students sold 350 bars. How much money was collected? How much of the money was profit?

Answer:

$_____ collected

$_____ profit

Daily Word Problems

Friday-Week 3

Student Council

Student council members want to buy playground equipment. They can buy a complete basketball set for $300 or they can buy the items separately.

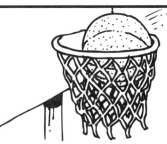

Complete Basketball Set

Set includes

Pole, Backboard, Net, and 4 Balls!

Only $300

Basketball Equipment

Pole $125

Backboard $45

Net $15

Basketballs $30 each

Which is the better deal? Explain why.

_____

_____

_____

_____

_____

Daily Word Problems

Monday–Week 4

Garden Shop

Olisa has a garden shop. One customer wants to buy 42 snapdragon plants. There are 6 snapdragons in a pack. How many packs should Olisa sell to her customer?

Name:

Work Space:

Answer:

_____ packs

Daily Word Problems

Tuesday–Week 4

Garden Shop

Olisa charges $12.00 an hour to fix lawn mowers. If Olisa works $2\frac{1}{4}$ hours on a lawn mower, how much should she charge?

Name:

Work Space:

Answer:

$ _____

Daily Word Problems

Wednesday-Week 4

Garden Shop

A customer wants to buy fertilizer spikes for her trees. Olisa knows that each tree will need a total of 6 spikes throughout the season. The customer has 17 trees. How many spikes should the customer buy? What is the total cost if each spike costs 50¢?

Name:

Work Space:

Answer:

_____ spikes

$_____ total cost

Daily Word Problems

Thursday-Week 4

Garden Shop

A customer wants to buy 60 flowering plants. He wants $\frac{1}{2}$ of them to be alyssum, $\frac{1}{4}$ of them to be bells of Ireland, and $\frac{1}{4}$ of them to be calendula. How many of each type of flower should Olisa sell to her customer?

Name:

Work Space:

Answer:

_____ alyssum

_____ bells of Ireland

_____ calendula

Daily Word Problems

Friday-Week 4

Name:

Garden Shop

A customer bought a cart full of flowering plants. Help Olisa complete the bill shown below. Remember to find the total.

Number of Plants	Type of Plant	Price for Each Plant	Price for All Plants
5	zinnia	$0.75	
4	wallflower	$0.95	
3	vinca	$0.85	
2	torenia	$0.99	
1	sweet pea	$1.05	
		Total	

Daily Word Problems

Monday-Week 5

Science Experiments

Students in Ms. Holloway's class were learning that two bits of matter, like marbles and water, cannot occupy the same space. She demonstrated this by dropping marbles into a jar that was filled with water. The level of the water rose from 55 milliliters to 72 milliliters. How much did the water level rise?

Name:

Work Space:

Answer:

_____ milliliters

Daily Word Problems

Tuesday-Week 5

Science Experiments

Ms. Holloway showed that some liquids are heavier than others. She poured molasses, water, and cooking oil into a jar. The liquids separated into 3 layers. If she poured 20 milliliters of molasses into the jar, how much water is in the jar? How much cooking oil is in the jar?

Name:

Work Space:

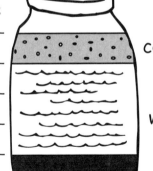

cooking oil

water

molasses

Answer:

_____ milliliters of water

_____ milliliters of cooking oil

Daily Word Problems

Wednesday-Week 5

Science Experiments

Ms. Holloway demonstrated how insulation can keep ice frozen longer. She wrapped 1 ice cube in cardboard and left another ice cube unwrapped. The unwrapped ice cube melted after 55 minutes. The insulated ice cube melted after 1 hour, 27 minutes. How much longer did it take for the insulated ice cube to melt?

Name:

Work Space:

Answer:

_____ minutes longer

Daily Word Problems

Thursday-Week 5

Science Experiments

To show that black paper absorbs more light waves than white paper, Ms. Holloway placed a thermometer covered with black paper and a thermometer covered with white paper under a 100-watt lamp. The thermometer under the black paper measured 84°; the one under the white paper measured 79°. How much hotter was the thermometer under the black paper?

Name:

Work Space:

Answer:

_____ ° hotter

Science Experiments

Ms. Holloway demonstrated evaporation— when a liquid becomes a gas. She poured 135 milliliters of water into a jar. Then the students measured how much water was left in the jar each day.

Water Left in the Jar

Day	Level of Water
1	135 ml
2	110 ml
3	73 ml
4	41 ml
5	0 ml

Use the chart to answer the following questions.

• How much water evaporated each day?

_____

_____

• On which day did the most water evaporate? The least?

_____   _____

• Estimate how many days it would take for 200 milliliters of water to evaporate. Explain why.

_____

_____

Daily Word Problems

Monday-Week 6

Swimming

Gail is on a swim team. Her best time for the 100-meter backstroke is 1 minute and 45 seconds. She just beat her best time by 9 seconds. What is her new best time?

Name:

Work Space:

Answer:

_____ minutes, _____ seconds

Daily Word Problems

Tuesday-Week 6

Swimming

Robert swims the 200-meter butterfly and the 150-meter freestyle at each swim meet. If he swims in 8 meets a year, how many meters will he swim?

Name:

Work Space:

Answer:

_____ meters

Daily Word Problems

Wednesday-Week 6

Swimming

Gail practices swimming for 1¼ hours every day. How much time does she practice in a week? In 5 weeks?

Name:

Work Space:

Answer:

_____ hours in 1 week

_____ hours in 5 weeks

Daily Word Problems

Thursday-Week 6

Swimming

Robert can swim the first 50 meters of a race in 1 minute. Then he slows down by 12 seconds for each of the next 50 meters of a race. How long will it take Robert to swim a 400-meter race?

Name:

Work Space:

Answer:

_____ minutes, _____ seconds

 Daily Word Problems • EMC 3004

Gail is on a 4-person freestyle relay team. The chart shows how fast each person on the team swims her leg of the race.

4-Person Freestyle Relay Team

Person	Time
Gail	1 minute, 15 seconds
Bonnie	1 minute, 18 seconds
Michelle	1 minute, 25 seconds
Jean	1 minute, 12 seconds

Use the chart to answer the following questions.

• How much faster is Jean's time than Gail's time?

_____

• How long will it take the team to finish the race?

_____

• The water was cold one day. This slowed everybody down by 3 seconds. How much slower was this race compared to their normal time?

_____

• If each swimmer improves her leg of the race by 4 seconds, what will their new overall time be?

_____

Daily Word Problems

Monday–Week 7

Baby-sitting

Ali baby-sits almost every weekend. This Friday night she will baby-sit from 6:00 p.m. to 9:00 p.m. She will be paid $3.50 an hour. How much money will she earn?

Name:

Work Space:

Answer:

$ _____

Daily Word Problems

Tuesday–Week 7

Baby-sitting

On Saturday night, Ali started to baby-sit at 5:30 p.m. She baby-sat for 3 hours and 10 minutes. What time was it when she was finished?

Name:

Work Space:

Answer:

_____ : _____ p.m.

Daily Word Problems

Wednesday–Week 7

Baby-sitting

One night Ali was paid $12.00 for baby-sitting from 5:00 p.m. to 8:00 p.m. How much was she paid for each hour?

Name:

Work Space:

Answer:

$_____ per hour

Daily Word Problems

Thursday–Week 7

Baby-sitting

Ali baby-sat 3 children from 10:30 a.m. to 3:00 p.m. She was paid $2.00 an hour for each child. How much money did she earn?

Name:

Work Space:

Answer:

$_____

Name:

Baby-sitting

- Ali makes about $23.00 baby-sitting each weekend.
  How much money will she make in a year? _____

- She puts half of what she makes in the bank.
  How much money will she have in the bank after 1 year? _____

The money that she doesn't put in the bank is her spending money. She made this list of things that she would like to buy.

CD player $40, camera $20, video game $20, CD $15, book $5

- List 3 different combinations of things that she can buy with her spending money after 4 weeks.

List 1	List 2	List 3

Daily Word Problems

Monday-Week 8

Edison

Thomas Alva Edison was one of the most important inventors in the United States. He invented the incandescent lamp, the phonograph, moving pictures, and much more. He was born in 1847 and died in 1931. How many years did he live?

Name:

Work Space:

Answer:

_____ years

Daily Word Problems

Tuesday-Week 8

Edison

Edison's first light bulb stayed lit for 40 hours. Today a typical light bulb can stay lit for 1,000 hours. How many of Edison's light bulbs would burn out before one of today's light bulbs burns out?

Name:

Work Space:

Answer:

_____ light bulbs

Daily Word Problems

Wednesday-Week 8

Edison

One of Edison's first cylinders for a phonograph could play for only 4 minutes. Today a compact disc can play for 72 minutes. How many 4-minute cylinders could be played in the same amount of time as one compact disc?

Name:

Work Space:

Answer:

_____ cylinders

Daily Word Problems

Thursday-Week 8

Edison

Edison's early films were shown on Kinetoscopes. Only one person could see the film at a time and it cost 5¢. Today a movie ticket can cost as much as $10. How many of Edison's films could a person watch for the price of a movie ticket today?

Name:

Work Space:

Answer:

_____ films

Name:

Some of Edison's first inventions were to improve the telegraph. He invented the automatic telegraph, duplex telegraph, and message printer. The telegraph allowed people to send messages by using short and long beeps. Different combinations of beeps represented letters and numbers. These different combinations of beeps are called Morse Code.

A	•—	S	•••
B	—•••	T	—
C	—•—•	U	••—
D	—••	V	•••—
E	•	W	•——
F	••—•	X	—••—
G	——•	Y	—•——
H	••••	Z	——••
I	••	1	•————
J	•———	2	••———
K	—•—	3	•••——
L	•—••	4	••••—
M	——	5	•••••
N	—•	6	—••••
O	———	7	——•••
P	•——•	8	———••
Q	——•—	9	————•
R	•—•	0	—————

Use the chart to write these numbers given in Morse Code.

•———— ••••• —•••• ————— _____

••——— •••—— •———— ——••• _____

————• ••••— ———•• ————— _____

——••• ••••• —•••• •———— —————— ••——— ———•• _____

_____

Daily Word Problems

Monday-Week 9

Fish Tank

Name:

Work Space:

Ken is setting up a tropical fish tank. He bought 5 angelfish for 50¢ each, 4 guppies for 40¢ each, and 3 neons for 30¢ each. How much money did Ken spend on the fish? How many fish did he buy?

Answer:

$_____

_____ fish

Daily Word Problems

Tuesday-Week 9

Fish Tank

Name:

Work Space:

Ken's fish tank cost $35.30. The air pump cost $12.50. The rocks for the floor of the tank cost $3.99. Fish food cost $4.25. How much money did Ken spend on these items?

Answer:

$_____

Daily Word Problems

Wednesday-Week 9

Fish Tank

Ken has good news: 4 of his 5 angelfish hatched babies! They each hatched 8 babies. How many babies were there in all? How many angelfish are in the tank now, including the adults?

Name:

Work Space:

Answer:

_____ babies in all

_____ angelfish in all

Daily Word Problems

Thursday-Week 9

Fish Tank

Ken wants to sell some of the baby angelfish when they are old enough. He wants to sell 24 of the angelfish for 40¢ each. If he sells all 24 of them, how much money will Ken receive? Ken sold only 23 of the fish. How much money did he receive?

Name:

Work Space:

Answer:

$_____ for 24 angelfish

$_____ for 23 angelfish

Name:

Ken wants to buy a larger tank so he can have more fish. The pet store manager said that 2 fish can live in 1 gallon of water, 5 fish in 2 gallons, 8 fish in 3 gallons, or 11 fish in 4 gallons.

Complete this chart to show how many fish can live in larger fish tanks.

Number of Gallons of Water	Number of Fish
1	2
2	5
3	8
4	11
5	
6	
7	
8	
9	
10	
15	
20	
30	
50	

Explain the rule you used to complete the pattern.

_____

_____

_____

_____

_____

_____

Daily Word Problems

Monday-Week 10

Time

Maggie had a school project to time different events. She found that her classmates took 1 minute and 12 seconds to line up for recess and 2 minutes and 20 seconds to line up after recess. How much longer did it take her classmates to line up after recess?

Name:

Work Space:

Answer:

_____ min(s)., _____ sec. longer

Daily Word Problems

Tuesday-Week 10

Time

Maggie timed how long it took her to finish a jigsaw puzzle. The first time she finished in 12 minutes. She was able to finish the puzzle twice as fast the second time and three times as fast the third time. How long did it take her to finish the puzzle the second and third times?

Name:

Work Space:

Answer:

_____ minutes the second time

_____ minutes the third time

Daily Word Problems
Wednesday-Week 10

Time

Maggie timed how long it took her pet mouse to go through a maze to find food. The first time the mouse found the food in 1 minute and 5 seconds, the second time in 55 seconds, and the third time in 45 seconds. Predict how fast the mouse will find the food a fourth time. Explain your answer.

Name:

Work Space:

Answer:

_____ seconds

_____

_____

_____

Daily Word Problems
Thursday-Week 10

Time

Maggie timed how long it takes her to shower in the morning. She uses $1\frac{1}{2}$ gallons of water for each minute that she showers. How much water will she use if her shower lasts 7 minutes?

Name:

Work Space:

Answer:

_____ gallons

Daily Word Problems

Friday-Week 10

Time

Maggie checked the reflexes of 10 students. First she held a ruler between the student's finger and thumb. Then she dropped the ruler and the student grabbed it. She recorded the results.

Student Reflexes

Student	A	B	C	D	E	F	G	H	I	J
Distance on Ruler	12 cm	10 cm	12 cm	8 cm	16 cm	10 cm	14 cm	12 cm	10 cm	12 cm

Students with the quickest reflexes had a shorter distance on the ruler.

Use the chart to answer the following questions.

• Which student or students had the quickest reflexes?

_____

• Which student or students had the slowest reflexes?

_____

• Which distance on the ruler did most students have?

_____

• If it takes 0.1 seconds for the ruler to drop 2 centimeters, what was the fastest time? The slowest time?

_____   _____

Daily Word Problems

Monday-Week 11

Making Sandwiches

Dan is making 30 sandwiches. Each sandwich will have 4 slices of turkey. Each package of turkey has 26 slices. How many packages of turkey will Dan need?

Name:

Work Space:

Answer:

_____ packages

Daily Word Problems

Tuesday-Week 11

Making Sandwiches

Dan needs to buy tomatoes to put on 30 turkey sandwiches. If the slices of one tomato can go on 4 sandwiches, how many tomatoes should he buy?

Name:

Work Space:

Answer:

_____ tomatoes

Daily Word Problems

Wednesday-Week 11

Making Sandwiches

Tomatoes cost $1.98 a pound. Explain how Dan can estimate the cost of 4 pounds of tomatoes without using paper or pencil. Then give the estimated cost.

Name:

Work Space:

Answer: _____

_____

_____

estimated cost: $_____

Daily Word Problems

Thursday-Week 11

Making Sandwiches

Dan needs to know how many loaves of bread to buy to make 30 sandwiches. If each sandwich has 2 slices of bread, and each loaf of bread has 18 slices, how many loaves should Dan buy? How many slices of bread are left over?

Name:

Work Space:

Answer:

_____ loaves

_____ slices left over

Name:

Making Sandwiches

Dan's sandwich business is going well. He wants to know how much profit he makes on each sandwich. He wrote down the cost of all the items that he uses in a sandwich.

> 2 slices of bread - 10¢ per slice
>
> 2 slices of tomato - 15¢ per slice
>
> 4 slices of turkey - 22¢ per slice
>
> mayonnaise - 8¢ per sandwich

• Dan charges $3.50 for each sandwich. Fill in the chart to show how much profit he will make.

Number of Sandwiches	Profit
1	
10	
50	

• If each slice of turkey goes up 3¢, how much profit will Dan make on each sandwich?

_____

Daily Word Problems

Monday-Week 12

Classroom Party

Ms. Holloway is having a classroom party. She asked her 27 students to help plan it. Ms. Holloway wants to give each student 15 jelly beans. How many jelly beans should she buy?

Name:

Work Space:

Answer:

_____ jelly beans

Daily Word Problems

Tuesday-Week 12

Classroom Party

Ms. Holloway has planned 4 different party activities for the class. Each one takes 25 minutes. If the party starts at 1:00 p.m., at what time will the party be over?

Name:

Work Space:

Answer:

_____ : _____ p.m.

Daily Word Problems

Wednesday-Week 12

Classroom Party

Ms. Holloway has 4 bags of miniature candy bars. Each bag contains 30 candy bars. How many candy bars will each of the 27 students receive? How many will be left over?

Name:

Work Space:

Answer:

_____ candy bars each

_____ left over

Daily Word Problems

Thursday-Week 12

Classroom Party

Ms. Holloway wants to know how much the party will cost. The drinks cost $7.25. The jelly beans cost $4.75. Each of the 4 bags of candy bars cost $3.50. What is the total cost for the party?

Name:

Work Space:

Answer:

$_____

Daily Word Problems

Name:

Classroom Party

Ms. Holloway has 3 secret numbers. Whoever guesses her secret numbers will win a prize at the party. Can you guess her numbers?

This number is a factor of 12.

There are three letters used to spell the name of this number.

It is a multiple of both 3 and 2.

This number is _____.

This number is a factor of 20.

It is less than 15 and greater than 3.

It is not an even number.

This number is _____.

This number is a factor of 40.

It is a multiple of both 2 and 5.

It is not a multiple of 4.

This number is _____.

38

Daily Word Problems

Monday-Week 13

Gleaning

Every fall Ms. Holloway's class gathers vegetables that stay in a field after the field has been harvested. This is called gleaning. The class plans to glean some fields for 2½ hours. If they start at 8:15 a.m., at what time will they be finished?

Name:

Work Space:

Answer:

_____ : _____ a.m.

Daily Word Problems

Tuesday-Week 13

Gleaning

Ms. Holloway's class gleaned an onion field. Each student gleaned an average of 9 pounds of onions. There are 27 students in the class. About how many pounds of onions did the whole class glean?

Name:

Work Space:

Answer:

_____ pounds

Daily Word Problems

Wednesday-Week 13

Gleaning

The students spent 2½ hours at the fields. During that time, they took 3 ten-minute breaks. How much time did students spend gleaning the fields?

Name:

Work Space:

Answer:

_____ hours

Daily Word Problems

Thursday-Week 13

Gleaning

Each of the 27 students gleaned about 18 pounds of carrots. About how many pounds of carrots did Ms. Holloway's class glean in all?

Name:

Work Space:

Answer:

_____ pounds

Daily Word Problems

Name:

Gleaning

Ms. Holloway's class also gleaned a potato field. This chart shows how many pounds of potatoes the students gleaned.

Pounds of Potatoes Gleaned

	10 pounds	11 pounds	12 pounds	13 pounds	14 pounds	15 pounds
Number of Students	4	6	5	8	3	1

Use the chart to answer the following questions.

• How many students gleaned more than 13 pounds of potatoes?

_____

• How many students gleaned fewer than 13 pounds of potatoes?

_____

• How many pounds of potatoes were gleaned in all?

_____

Daily Word Problems

Monday–Week 14

Breakfast Facts

Name:

Work Space:

Sally eats 2 ounces of cereal for breakfast each day. How many ounces of cereal does she eat in 1 week? How many ounces of cereal does she eat in 30 days?

Answer:

_____ ounces in 1 week

_____ ounces in 30 days

Daily Word Problems

Tuesday–Week 14

Breakfast Facts

Name:

Work Space:

Sally's mother buys milk in a one-quart container. Sally drinks 1 cup of milk each morning. How many days can Sally drink a cup of milk before her mother has to buy a new container?

| 2 cups = 1 pint |
| 2 pints = 1 quart |

Answer:

_____ days

Daily Word Problems

Wednesday-Week 14

Breakfast Facts

Sally loves pancakes. She ate 10 silver dollar-sized pancakes on Monday, 9 on Tuesday, 8 on Wednesday, and so on through Sunday. How many pancakes did she eat in all from Monday through Sunday?

Name:

Work Space:

Answer:

_____ pancakes

Daily Word Problems

Thursday-Week 14

Breakfast Facts

Sally ate breakfast at a restaurant. Sally ordered a muffin and egg sandwich for $2.50, hash brown potatoes for $1.25, and orange juice for 75¢. Her mother told her that she could spend $5.00. Did she have enough money to buy milk for 50¢? Explain why she did or did not have enough money.

Name:

Work Space:

Answer: _____

_____

_____

_____

Daily Word Problems

Name:

Breakfast Facts

Sally went to the store to buy cereal. The store had two brands of her favorite cereal, corn flakes.

Box A	Box B

 Corn Flakes
20 ounces

$3.00

 Corn Flakes
30 ounces

$3.60

• Which box has the best value? Explain why.

_____

_____

• Sally can use a 75¢-off coupon if she buys two 20-ounce boxes of corn flakes. How much would she spend on the two boxes if she uses the coupon?

_____

• Sally saw this sign in the store for corn flakes. How much would she spend on two 30-ounce boxes of corn flakes?

_____

Buy 1 30-ounce box of corn flakes and get the next box at half price.

Daily Word Problems

Monday-Week 15

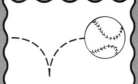

Physics
Demonstrations

Name:

Work Space:

Ms. Holloway explained that buoyancy is when an object, like a boat, floats in a liquid. She made a boat out of aluminum foil. She placed 34 paper clips, each weighing 12 grams, into the boat before it sank. How much weight did the boat hold before it sank?

Answer:

_____ grams

Daily Word Problems

Tuesday-Week 15

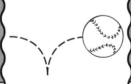

Physics
Demonstrations

Name:

Work Space:

Ms. Holloway's students measured the length of their shadows at different times of the day. Jeb's shadow was 37 inches longer in the morning than it was at lunchtime. If his shadow measured 51 inches long in the morning, how long was his shadow at lunchtime?

Answer:

_____ inches

Daily Word Problems

Wednesday-Week 15

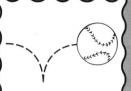

Physics Demonstrations

Ms. Holloway demonstrated that temperature affects how high a ball will bounce. A warm ball bounced 102 cm high. A cold ball bounced 84 cm high. How much higher did the warm ball bounce?

Name:

Work Space:

Answer:

_____ cm higher

Daily Word Problems

Thursday-Week 15

Physics Demonstrations

Ms. Holloway's students tested how far paper airplanes can fly. Matt's plane flew 8 m, 45 cm; Ted's plane flew 7 m, 55 cm; Maggie's plane flew 9 m, 30 cm; and MaryAnn's plane flew 7 m, 90 cm. What is the difference between the longest and shortest flights?

Name:

Work Space:

Answer:

_____ m, _____ cm difference

Daily Word Problems

Name:

Physics Demonstrations

Ms. Holloway rolled a ball down a ramp. Then she placed different materials on the ramp to demonstrate how friction can make the ball roll slower. The students timed how long it took the ball to roll down the ramp with each kind of material.

Friction Demonstration

Material	Time (in seconds)
notebook paper	4.25
sandpaper	4.37
cotton cloth	4.4
wool cloth	4.92
thin carpet	5.02
thick carpet	5.9

Use the chart to answer the following questions.

• Which kind of material allowed the ball to roll down the ramp in the shortest amount of time?

_____

• How much longer did the ball take to roll down the ramp with thick carpet than with thin carpet?

_____

• If you wanted the ball to roll down the ramp in less than 4.5 seconds, which kinds of material could you use on the ramp?

_____

• Ms. Holloway used a ramp that was twice as long. Predict how long it would take the ball to roll down this ramp if it was covered with thin carpet.

_____

Daily Word Problems

Monday-Week 16

Bulletin Board

Ms. Holloway is putting up a bulletin board about frogs. The bulletin board is 6 feet wide and 4 feet tall. She wants to put a border around the board. What is the distance around the edge of the bulletin board?

Name:

Work Space:

Answer:

_____ feet

Daily Word Problems

Tuesday-Week 16

Bulletin Board

The bulletin board is 6 feet wide and 4 feet tall. The border is 3 inches wide. What are the dimensions inside the border?

Name:

Work Space:

Answer:

_____

Daily Word Problems

Wednesday-Week 16

Bulletin Board

Ms. Holloway has 3 pictures of frogs to put on the bulletin board. Each picture measures 10 inches by 10 inches. If the bulletin board is 6 feet by 4 feet and the border is 3 inches wide, will all 3 pictures fit on the bulletin board?

Name:

Work Space:

Answer:

_____

Daily Word Problems

Thursday-Week 16

Bulletin Board

Ms. Holloway is putting this title on the bulletin board: "Jump Right into Learning About Frogs." Each capital letter is 1½ inches wide, lowercase letters are 1 inch wide, and there is a 1-inch space between words. How long will the title be?

Name:

Work Space:

Jump Right into Learning About Frogs

Answer:

_____ inches

Daily Word Problems

Bulletin Board

Name:

Decorate your own bulletin board on the grid below. Use the scale to draw the following pictures on the bulletin board. (You may turn the pictures if you'd like.)

- 9 inches by 12 inches
- 15 inches by 18 inches
- 18 inches by 24 inches

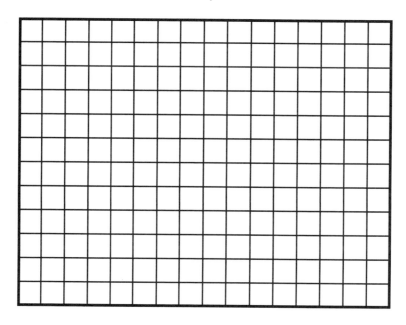

Scale:
Each ☐ represents 3 inches by 3 inches

- What are the actual dimensions of the bulletin board in feet?

  _____

- What is the distance around the bulletin board in feet?

  _____

                   Daily Word Problems • EMC 3004

Daily Word Problems

Monday-Week 17

Mountains

The tallest mountain in the world, Mount Everest, is 29,035 feet high. The tallest mountain in the United States, Mount McKinley, is 20,320 feet high. How much taller is Mount Everest than Mount McKinley?

Name:

Work Space:

Answer:

_____ feet

Daily Word Problems

Tuesday-Week 17

Mountains

A guide climbs a mountain at the rate of 30 minutes for every 50 feet. How many hours will it take the guide to climb 750 feet?

Name:

Work Space:

Answer:

_____ hours

Daily Word Problems

Wednesday-Week 17

Mountains

A volcanic mountain in the Pacific Ocean is 13,796 feet above sea level. The mountain extends 18,200 feet from sea level down to the ocean floor. How tall is the mountain from the ocean floor to the summit?

Name:

Work Space:

Answer:

_____ feet

Daily Word Problems

Thursday-Week 17

Mountains

A mountain climber drinks a 32-ounce bottle of water every 90 minutes on a hike. How many water bottles should the mountain climber bring on a hike that lasts 4 hours and 30 minutes?

Name:

Work Space:

Answer:

_____ bottles

Name:

There are five vegetation zones in the Rocky Mountains:

Plains, below 5,400 feet

Foothills, 5,400–7,000 feet

Montane, 7,000–9,000 feet

Subalpine, 9,000–11,500 feet

Alpine, above 11,500 feet

While on a hike, several living things were observed at different altitudes. List the vegetation zone for each living thing.

Living Things Observed on a Hike

Living Thing	Altitude (in feet)	Vegetation Zone
Sagebrush	6,045	
Englemann spruce	9,300	
Juniper	5,506	
Lodgepole pine	8,542	
Aspen	7,433	
Ground-hugging flower	13,045	
Rocky Mountain goat	9,040	
Bighorn sheep	8,502	
Coyote	6,800	

Daily Word Problems

Monday-Week 18

4-H

Trevor is a member of 4-H, a club that helps students learn about farming. His 4-H project was to raise a pig and then sell it at auction. Trevor bought a pig that weighed 56 pounds and cost $3 a pound. How much did Trevor pay for his pig?

Name:

Work Space:

Answer:

$_____

Daily Word Problems

Tuesday-Week 18

4-H

Shelley bought a piglet for $139. She fed the piglet grain that cost a total of $56. Then she sold the pig at auction for $451. How much profit did Shelley earn?

Name:

Work Space:

Answer:

$_____ profit

Daily Word Problems

Wednesday-Week 18

4-H

Cody raises chickens so he can sell the eggs. Each of his 36 hens lays an average of 1 egg a week. How many dozen eggs should Cody have in 1 week? In 3 weeks? In 10 weeks?

Name:

Work Space:

Answer:

_____ dozen eggs in 1 week

_____ dozen eggs in 3 weeks

_____ dozen eggs in 10 weeks

Daily Word Problems

Thursday-Week 18

4-H

Eric has planted corn on 480 acres of land. Eric's harvesting machine, or combine, can harvest 80 acres a day. How many days will it take for Eric to harvest all 480 acres of corn? How many days would it take Eric to harvest his corn if he had 2 combines?

Name:

Work Space:

Answer:

_____ days to harvest 480 acres

_____ days using 2 combines

Name:

4-H

The Future Farmers Club has four members. Each decided to plant his or her favorite vegetable. Use the clues below to determine who grew each vegetable.

When you know that a vegetable is **not** grown by someone, make an **X** under that vegetable and across from that person's name.

When you know that a vegetable **is** grown by a person, write **YES** in that box. You can then **X** that vegetable for all the other people **and X** all the other vegetables for that person.

	Tomatoes	Beans	Carrots	Lettuce
Edward				
Lisa				
Ben				
Lara				

1. Edward grows a root vegetable.

2. Lara grows a green vegetable.

3. Ben uses his crop to make lots of spaghetti sauce.

4. Lisa's vegetable is most often cooked.

Daily Word Problems

Monday-Week 19

Astronomy

Ms. Holloway demonstrated why the poles of Earth are cold. She placed one thermometer close to a lamp and another thermometer several feet away. The thermometer closer to the lamp measured 95.5 degrees. The thermometer farther away measured 76.2 degrees. How much cooler was the distant thermometer?

Name:

Work Space:

Answer:

_____ degrees cooler

Daily Word Problems

Tuesday-Week 19

Astronomy

The Sun has a diameter of 864,000 miles. Venus has a diameter of 7,520 miles. How much larger is the Sun's diameter than Venus's diameter?

Name:

Work Space:

Answer:

_____ miles larger

Daily Word Problems

Wednesday-Week 19

Astronomy

Earth is about 93 million miles from the Sun. Neptune is about 3,006 million miles from the Sun. About how much farther is Neptune from the Sun than Earth?

Name:

Work Space:

Answer:

_____ million miles

Daily Word Problems

Thursday-Week 19

Astronomy

The Sun's diameter is about 860,000 miles. Earth's diameter is about 8,000 miles. Estimate how many times larger the Sun's diameter is than Earth's diameter.

Name:

Work Space:

Answer:

_____ times larger

Daily Word Problems

Friday-Week 19

Name:

Astronomy

This chart shows planetary rotations, the amount of time a planet takes to spin once on its axis.

Planetary Rotations

Planet	Mercury	Venus	Earth	Mars	Jupiter	Saturn	Uranus	Neptune
Rotation Time	58.6 days	243 days	1 day	24.6 hours	9.9 hours	10.2 hours	17.4 hours	16 hours

Use the chart to answer the following questions.

• Which planets have a rotation time that is longer than Earth's?

_____

• Which planet has the longest rotation time? The shortest rotation time?

_____   _____

• How much longer is the rotation time for Mars than for Earth?

_____

• How much longer is the rotation time for Venus than for Earth?

_____

Daily Word Problems

Monday-Week 20

U.S. Statistics

The area of our largest state, Alaska, is 615,230 square miles. The area of our smallest state, Rhode Island, is 1,231 square miles. How much larger is Alaska than Rhode Island?

Name:

Work Space:

Answer:

_____ square miles larger

Daily Word Problems

Tuesday-Week 20

U.S. Statistics

There were 696,115 people living in New York City in 1850. There were 7,195,842 more people living there in 1950. How many people lived in New York City in 1950?

Name:

Work Space:

Answer:

_____ people

 Daily Word Problems • EMC 3004

Daily Word Problems

Wednesday–Week 20

U.S. Statistics

In 1850 the city of San Francisco had a population of about 35,000 people. The city had about 10 times that many people living there in 1900. About how many people lived in San Francisco in 1900?

Name:

Work Space:

Answer:

_____ people

Daily Word Problems

Thursday–Week 20

U.S. Statistics

The city of Fort Wayne, Indiana, had a population of 4,282 in 1850 and 45,115 in 1900. The city of Montgomery, Alabama, had a population of 8,728 in 1850 and 30,346 in 1900. Which city's population increased more between 1850 and 1900? Explain your answer.

Name:

Work Space:

Answer: _____

_____

_____

_____

Daily Word Problems

U.S. Statistics

The number of people in the United States who are 85 and older has increased over the years.

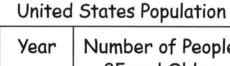

United States Population

Year	Number of People 85 and Older
1950	577,000
1960	929,000
1970	1,409,000
1980	2,240,000
1990	3,021,000

Use the chart to answer the following questions.

• By how much did the population increase each decade?

_____

_____

_____

• Between which two time periods was there the smallest increase in population? The largest increase?

_____   _____

• Predict how many people 85 and older there were in the year 2000 and how many there will be in 2010.

_____   _____

Daily Word Problems

Monday–Week 21

Hoover Dam

Hoover Dam is a magnificent structure standing 726 feet tall. Comparing the dam to the stories in a skyscraper is one way to visualize how tall the dam is. Each story in a typical skyscraper is 12 feet tall. How many skyscraper stories tall is Hoover Dam?

Name:

Work Space:

Answer:

_____ stories tall

Daily Word Problems

Tuesday–Week 21

Hoover Dam

Hoover Dam has 17 generators. If each generator produces 117 megawatts of electricity, how many megawatts in all do the generators produce?

Name:

Work Space:

Answer:

_____ megawatts

Daily Word Problems

Wednesday—Week 21

Hoover Dam

Hoover Dam weighs about six million, six hundred thousand tons. Write this number.

Name:

Work Space:

Answer:

_____

Daily Word Problems

Thursday—Week 21

Hoover Dam

Almost 30,000 people visit Hoover Dam each day. About how many people visit the dam each week?

Name:

Work Space:

Answer:

_____ people

Daily Word Problems

Name:

Hoover Dam

The table below shows lakes created by dams. Lake Mead contains 28,255,000 acre-feet of water. Figure out how much smaller the other lakes are compared to Lake Mead.

Size of Lakes/Reservoirs Created by Dams

Dam	Lake	Size of Lake in Acre-feet	Smaller Than Lake Mead by:
Glen Canyon	Powell	27,000,000	
Oahe	Oahe	19,300,000	
Garrison	Sakakawea	18,500,000	
Fort Peck	Fort Peck	15,400,000	
Grand Coulee	F.D. Roosevelt	9,562,000	
Libby	Koocanusa	5,809,000	

LAKE MEAD
28,255,000 acre-feet

Daily Word Problems • EMC 3004

Daily Word Problems

Monday-Week 22

Fun Park

Four friends, Abe, Bob, Carl, and Darrell, are going to a fun park. They want to ride the go-carts. The price to ride the go-carts is $2.15 for 5 minutes, $4.00 for 10 minutes, or $6.75 for 15 minutes. Which price is the best deal? Explain why.

Name:

Work Space:

Answer: _____

_____

_____

_____

Daily Word Problems

Tuesday-Week 22

Fun Park

The four friends want to know how many miles they drove on the go-cart track. The track is $\frac{3}{4}$ of a mile long. Each person went around the track 12 times. How many miles did each person drive? How many miles in all did the four friends drive?

Name:

Work Space:

Answer:

_____ miles each

_____ miles in all

Daily Word Problems

Wednesday-Week 22

Fun Park

The four friends want to play video games. Together they have a total of $8 to spend. Each game costs 25¢. How many games will each person be able to play?

Name:

Work Space:

Answer:

_____ games each

Daily Word Problems

Thursday-Week 22

Fun Park

Abe's video game score was 524 points. Bob's score was half as much as Abe's. Carl's score was twice as much as Abe's score. Darren's score was three times as much as Bob's. What scores did Bob, Carl, and Darren have?

Name:

Work Space:

Answer:

Bob's score was _____ points.

Carl's score was _____ points.

Darren's score was _____ points.

Daily Word Problems

Friday-Week 22

Fun Park

Carl played a ball toss game. The target shows where each ball landed.

```
        25
       50
      75
    100
```

- Add up Carl's score.

_____

- He can buy a prize with his total points. What is the highest-point prize that he can buy?

Points	Prizes
1000	baseball cap
900	stuffed animal
800	kite
700	bottle of bubbles
600	bag of marbles
500	high-bouncing ball

_____

Daily Word Problems
Monday-Week 23

Music

In 1994 The Rolling Stones rock band received $121.2 million for their North American concert tour. In 1998 Elton John received $46.2 million for his concert tour. How much more money did The Rolling Stones receive than Elton John?

Name:

Work Space:

Answer:

$_____ million more

Daily Word Problems
Tuesday-Week 23

Music

In 1991, 333.3 million music compact discs were shipped in the United States. There were twice as many discs shipped in 1994 and 3 times as many in 1999. How many discs were shipped in 1994 and in 1999?

Name:

Work Space:

Answer:

_____ million discs in 1994

_____ million discs in 1999

Daily Word Problems

Wednesday-Week 23

Music

In 1990 there were 442.2 million music cassettes shipped in the United States. Half as many cassettes were shipped in 1996 and $\frac{1}{3}$ as many in 1998. About how many cassettes were shipped in 1996 and in 1998?

Name:

Work Space:

Answer:

_____ million cassettes in 1996

_____ million cassettes in 1998

Daily Word Problems

Thursday-Week 23

Music

In 1999 there were more country music radio stations in the United States than any other type. Classical music had the fewest with 38 stations. If there were about 60 times as many country music stations as classical stations, about how many country stations were there?

Name:

Work Space:

Answer:

about _____ country music stations

Daily Word Problems

Music

The Stone Water Connection, a local rock band in Greeley, Colorado, began selling a compact disc of their latest concert. Each disc cost $3.75 to make and sold for $9.00.

Complete this chart to show the total number of CDs and how much profit the band made over a 4-week period.

The Stone Water Connection CD Sales

Week	Number of CDs	Profit for the Week
1	23	
2	17	
3	10	
4	16	
Total		

Daily Word Problems

Monday-Week 24

Earth Science

During an earth science unit, Ms. Holloway demonstrated the extreme amount of pressure needed to fold the earth's crust. She had each student fold a whole newspaper in half, as many times as possible. By the seventh fold, the newspaper couldn't be folded any more. How many layers of newspaper were there after the seventh fold?

Name:

Work Space:

Answer:

_____ layers

Daily Word Problems

Tuesday-Week 24

Earth Science

The Richter Scale is used to measure the strength of earthquakes. The higher the number is on the scale, the stronger the earthquake. Put these earthquakes in order from low to high on the Richter Scale.

Name:

Work Space:

1985	Michoacan, MX	8.1
1906	San Francisco, CA	7.7
1923	Yokohama, Japan	8.3
1994	Northridge, CA	6.8
1995	Kobe, Japan	6.9

Answer:

low 1._____

2. _____

3. _____

4. _____

high 5. _____

Daily Word Problems

Wednesday-Week 24

Earth Science

The greatest recorded depth of the Antarctic ice sheet was recorded at 15,400 feet. A mile is 5,280 feet. Estimate how many miles thick the ice is. Then explain how you made your estimate.

Name:

Work Space:

Answer:

about _____ miles thick

_____

_____

_____

Daily Word Problems

Thursday-Week 24

Earth Science

The average annual precipitation in Reno, Nevada, is 7.53 inches. The average for Honolulu, Hawaii, is 14.49 inches more than Reno. What is the average annual precipitation in Honolulu, Hawaii?

Name:

Work Space:

Answer:

_____ inches

Daily Word Problems

Name:

Earth Science

This chart shows the Fujita Scale that is used to measure damaging winds.

Fujita Scale for Damaging Winds

Scale	Wind Speed (in mph)	Damage
0	40–72	Light
1	73–112	Moderate
2	113–157	Considerable
3	158–206	Severe
4	207–260	Devastating
5	261–318	Incredible

Use the chart to answer the following questions.

• What Fujita Scale number would be given to a 245-mph wind?
  A 99-mph wind?

  _____   _____

• What type of damage would be done by a 214-mph wind?

  _____

Daily Word Problems

Monday-Week 25

Sharks

The whale shark can be as much as 50 feet long. The cigar shark is rarely more than 8 inches in length as an adult. How many cigar sharks would you need to put head to tail to match the length of a 50-foot whale shark?

Name:

Work Space:

Answer:

_____ cigar sharks

Daily Word Problems

Tuesday-Week 25

Sharks

Sharks lose teeth all the time. Each lost tooth, however, is quickly replaced. If a shark replaces an average of 4 teeth a week, how many teeth will be replaced in a year?

Name:

Work Space:

Answer:

_____ teeth

Daily Word Problems

Wednesday-Week 25

Sharks

The blue shark can swim at a speed of 40 miles per hour. If the shark swam at this speed for 15 minutes, how far would it swim? How long would it take the shark to travel 90 miles?

Name:

Work Space:

Answer:

_____ miles

_____ hours, _____ minutes

Daily Word Problems

Thursday-Week 25

Sharks

People all around the world eat shark steaks. Shark steaks can cost as much as $15 a pound. How much would a $3\frac{1}{4}$-pound shark steak cost?

Name:

Work Space:

Answer:

$_____

Name:

Sharks

The record weights of different types of sharks that have been caught off the New England coast are shown below.

Mako	1,115 lbs
Thresher	767 lbs
Porbeagle	507 lbs
Blue	454 lbs

Use the chart to answer the following questions.

• How much more does each one of these sharks weigh than a student who weighs 60 pounds?

Mako   _____

Thresher   _____

Porbeagle   _____

Blue   _____

• About how many 60-pound fourth-graders would equal the weight of each of these sharks?

Mako   _____

Thresher   _____

Porbeagle   _____

Blue   _____

Daily Word Problems

Monday-Week 26

Friends

A group of friends were throwing a football. Opie threw the ball 22.4 meters, Cam threw it 25.9 meters, Adam threw it 27.3 meters, Bo threw it 23.8 meters, and Dana threw it 30 meters. How much farther did Dana throw the football than each of her friends?

Name:

Work Space:

Answer:

_____ meters more than Opie

_____ meters more than Cam

_____ meters more than Adam

_____ meters more than Bo

Daily Word Problems

Tuesday-Week 26

Friends

A group of friends collected food for their town's food bank. Opie collected 7.9 pounds, Adam collected 12.2 pounds, Dana collected 8.3 pounds, Bo collected 6.9 pounds, and Cam collected 13.3 pounds. How many pounds of food did they collect in all?

Name:

Work Space:

Answer:

_____ pounds

Daily Word Problems

Wednesday-Week 26

Friends

Opie has 15 baseball cards. Adam has 3 times as many cards as Opie. Dana has 2 times as many as Opie. Bo has 4 times as many as Opie. Cam has 7 times as many as Opie. How many cards does each person have?

Name:

Work Space:

Answer:

Opie has _____ cards.

Adam has _____ cards.

Dana has _____ cards.

Bo has _____ cards.

Cam has _____ cards.

Daily Word Problems

Thursday-Week 26

Friends

A group of 5 friends put their money together, hoping that they could all go to the movies. This is how much they gave: $7.25, $5.50, $8.10, $3.25, and $6.90. If a movie ticket costs $6.00, will they have enough money? Explain why.

Name:

Work Space:

Answer: _____

_____

_____

_____

Daily Word Problems

Name:

Friends

Six friends sat around a table to work on a science project. They left an empty chair for Hector who had gone to gather supplies.

Use the clues to find out where each person sat.

1. Maria is seated between Ahmed and Felicia.

2. Tiffany is at the end of the table.

3. Ahmed is seated near Tiffany's left hand.

4. Frank is next to the empty chair.

5. Morgan is seated near Frank's left hand.

Daily Word Problems

Monday–Week 27

Biology

Ms. Holloway demonstrated how greenhouses help plants grow faster. She placed a glass jar over a patch of grass. A week later, the grass inside the jar was 15 millimeters longer than the grass growing outside the jar. If the grass outside the jar was 55 millimeters long, how long was the grass inside the jar?

Name:

Work Space:

Answer:

_____ millimeters

Daily Word Problems

Tuesday–Week 27

Biology

Ms. Holloway's students collected data on wildflower plants found on 5 square meters of prairie land. Maria found 17 gumweed, 33 black-eyed Susans, 27 common milkweed, 42 prairie rose, and 29 Indian paintbrush. How many more prairie rose and black-eyed Susans combined were there than common milkweed and gumweed combined?

Name:

Work Space:

Answer:

_____ more

Daily Word Problems

Wednesday-Week 27

Biology

Ms. Holloway's class started an earthworm farm with 7 worms. If at the end of each week there were twice as many worms as the week before, how many worms would there be after 4 weeks? After 8 weeks?

Name:

Work Space:

Answer:

_____ worms after 4 weeks

_____ worms after 8 weeks

Daily Word Problems

Thursday-Week 27

Biology

Ms. Holloway's class is learning about spiders. A single spider egg sac can hold as many as 3,000 eggs. If you found 7 egg sacs, how many eggs could there be in all? In 12 egg sacs?

Name:

Work Space:

Answer:

_____ eggs in 7 sacs

_____ eggs in 12 sacs

Name:

Ms. Holloway's class demonstrated how walking increases a person's heart rate. They made this line graph to show Ben's heart rate.

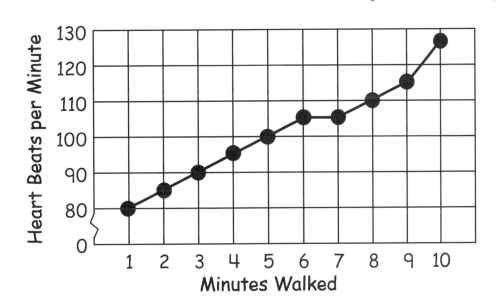

Use the graph to answer the following questions.

• After 1 minute, what was Ben's heart rate?

_____

• After 5 minutes, what was Ben's heart rate?

_____

• Ben's heart rate stayed the same between which 2 minutes of walking?

_____

• Between which 2 minutes of walking did Ben's heart rate increase the most?

_____

Daily Word Problems

Monday–Week 28

Weather

Through 1999 the lowest recorded temperature in Hawaii was 12 degrees. The highest recorded temperature was 100 degrees. How much warmer was the highest temperature than the lowest temperature?

Name:

Work Space:

Answer:

_____ degrees warmer

Daily Word Problems

Tuesday–Week 28

Weather

If snow is falling at a rate of $\frac{1}{4}$ inch every 30 minutes, how much snow will fall in $4\frac{1}{2}$ hours?

Name:

Work Space:

Answer:

_____ inches

Daily Word Problems

Wednesday-Week 28

Weather

Lima, Peru, receives an average of only 0.2 inch of rain a year. How many years of rain must fall in Lima to match the annual rainfall of 14.6 inches in Athens, Greece?

Name:

Work Space:

Answer:

_____ years

Daily Word Problems

Thursday-Week 28

Weather

If the daytime high temperature was 76 degrees above zero and then dropped 40 degrees that night, what would be the temperature then?

Name:

Work Space:

Answer:

_____ degrees

 Daily Word Problems • EMC 3004

Daily Word Problems

Name:

Weather

Ed started a sidewalk snow-removal business. It takes him 20 minutes to clear each inch of snow that falls on an average sidewalk.

Complete the chart below to show how long each snow-removal job will take. Change the time to hours and minutes whenever possible.

Snow in Inches	Time to Remove the Snow
2	
2.5	
5	
6.25	
10	

Daily Word Problems

Monday-Week 29

Trains

In 1829, the Rocket, a steam locomotive, had a top speed of 29 mph. Today, the French train TGV can travel at a speed of up to 238 mph. How much faster is the TGV than the Rocket?

Name:

Work Space:

Answer:

_____ mph faster

Daily Word Problems

Tuesday-Week 29

Trains

The Japanese Bullet train takes only 3 hours to travel from Tokyo to Osaka, a distance of 321 miles. What is the average speed of the train during this trip?

Name:

Work Space:

Answer:

_____ mph

Daily Word Problems

Wednesday—Week 29

Trains

The four longest railway tunnels in the world are Seikan, in Japan, 33.5 miles; Simplon No. 1 and 2, in Switzerland and Italy, 12 miles; the English Channel Tunnel, 31 miles; and Dai-shimizu, in Japan, 14 miles. What is the difference in length between the longest and the shortest of these tunnels?

Name:

Work Space:

Answer:

_____ miles difference

Daily Word Problems

Thursday—Week 29

Trains

A train is traveling from Albuquerque, New Mexico, to Denver, Colorado, 480 miles away. The train travels 60 miles an hour. The train will make one 30-minute stop to pick up passengers. If the train leaves the station at 8 a.m., at what time will it arrive in Denver?

Name:

Work Space:

Answer:

_____ : _____ p.m.

Name:

This chart shows the railroad distances from Albuquerque, New Mexico, to different cities in the United States.

Distance from Albuquerque, New Mexico

City	Distance in Miles
Amarillo, Texas	374
Baltimore, Maryland	2,102
Buffalo, New York	1,862
Cheyenne, Wyoming	583
Denver, Colorado	480
Fargo, North Dakota	1,605
Kansas City, Missouri	887
Los Angeles, California	889
Miami, Florida	2,185
Omaha, Nebraska	1,015
Salt Lake City, Utah	985
Tucson, Arizona	585

Use the chart to answer the following questions.

• Which city is the closest to Albuquerque?   _____

• Which city is the farthest from Albuquerque?   _____

• How many fewer miles are there when traveling from Albuquerque to Denver, than from Albuquerque to Miami?   _____

• How many more miles are there when traveling from Albuquerque to Buffalo, than from Albuquerque to Tucson?   _____

Daily Word Problems

Monday-Week 30

Television

In 1980, 82% of all households in the United States had a color television set. In 1998, 99% of all households in the United States had a color television set. What percent did not have a color television set in 1980? What percent did not have a color television set in 1998?

Name:

Work Space:

Answer:

_____% had no color TV in 1980

_____% had no color TV in 1998

Daily Word Problems

Tuesday-Week 30

Television

In 1977, 17% of all United States households had cable television. In 1998, 67% had cable television. How much did the percentage of households that had cable increase from 1977 to 1998? How many years were in this study?

Name:

Work Space:

Answer:

_____% increase

_____ years in the study

Daily Word Problems

Wednesday-Week 30

Television

If a person watches 35 hours of television each week, how many hours of television would that person watch in a year? **Challenge:** How many days would that be?

Name:

Work Space:

Answer:

_____ hours in a year

_____ days, _____ hours

Daily Word Problems

Thursday-Week 30

Television

In 1999 children aged 6 to 11 watched television an average of $10\frac{1}{2}$ hours a week. If those same children spent 30 minutes each night, Monday through Thursday, working on homework, how much time was spent on homework each week? How much more time was spent watching television?

Name:

Work Space:

Answer:

_____ hours a week on homework

_____ more hours watching TV

Daily Word Problems

Name:

Television

On the chart below, record how much time you spent watching television and how much time you spent working on homework over the past week.

Day	Time Watching TV	Time Working on Homework
Sunday		
Monday		
Tuesday		
Wednesday		
Thursday		
Friday		
Saturday		
Total		

When the chart is completed, answer the following questions.

• Did you watch television more or less than $10\frac{1}{2}$ hours a week? How much more or less?

_____

• Did you work on homework more or less than $2\frac{1}{2}$ hours a week? How much more or less?

_____

Daily Word Problems

Monday-Week 31

Animals

Darrell was reading about elephants. He learned that African elephants can be 13 feet tall at the shoulders and weigh 15,400 pounds. How much taller and heavier is an African elephant than a student who is 4 feet, 5 inches tall and weighs 72 pounds?

Name:

Work Space:

Answer:

_____ feet, _____ inches taller

_____ pounds heavier

Daily Word Problems

Tuesday-Week 31

Animals

Darrell learned that an Asian elephant can live an average of 40 years. How many times longer is that compared to a guinea pig's 4 years? A domestic rabbit's 5 years? A giraffe's 10 years? A baboon's 20 years?

Name:

Work Space:

Answer:

_____ times longer than a guinea pig

_____ times longer than a rabbit

_____ times longer than a giraffe

_____ times longer than a baboon

Daily Word Problems

Wednesday-Week 31

Animals

Darrell learned that elephants in the wild can eat 165 to 330 pounds of plants each day. How many pounds of food is that in a week?

Name:

Work Space:

Answer:

_____ to _____ pounds per week

Daily Word Problems

Thursday-Week 31

Animals

Jenny learned that kangaroos can jump about 16 feet. During the 1996 Summer Olympics, Chioma Ajunwa from Nigeria received the gold medal for reaching 23 feet, $4\frac{1}{2}$ inches in the long jump. How much farther did Chioma Ajunwa jump than a kangaroo?

Name:

Work Space:

Answer:

_____ feet, _____ inches farther

Name:

MaryAnn is learning about cheetahs. She discovered that a cheetah's top running speed is 70 miles per hour. She wanted to compare this to other animals. This chart shows the top speeds of cheetahs and other animals in the world.

Animal	Top Speed (in mph)
Black mamba snake	20
Cheetah	70
Chicken	9
Greyhound	39
Lion	50
Pronghorn antelope	61
Warthog	30
Zebra	40

Use the chart to answer the following questions.

• Which animal or animals have a top speed that is more than three times as fast as a black mamba snake?

_____

• About how many times faster is a cheetah than a chicken?

_____

• If these animals were in a race, which animal would finish first? Fifth? Last?

_____   _____   _____

Daily Word Problems

Monday-Week 32

Quilts

Each square of Jacob's quilt has 4 triangles. His quilt has 9 squares across the length and 9 squares across the width of the quilt. How many triangles are in the quilt?

Name:

Work Space:

Answer:

_____ triangles

Daily Word Problems

Tuesday-Week 32

Quilts

Julie's quilt measures 72 inches by 80 inches. There are 9 squares across the width and 10 squares across the length of her quilt. What are the dimensions of each square?

Name:

Work Space:

Answer:

_____ inches by _____ inches

Daily Word Problems

Wednesday-Week 32

Quilts

Audrey is making a quilt. Each square of the quilt is 10 inches by 10 inches. There are 8 squares across the length and 8 squares across the width of the quilt. What is the length and width of the quilt in feet and inches? What is the perimeter of the quilt?

Name:

Work Space:

Answer:

length = _____ ft., _____ in.

width = _____ ft., _____ in.

perimeter = _____ ft., _____ in.

Daily Word Problems

Thursday-Week 32

Quilts

Lee's quilt has 8 squares across the length and the width. If each square of the quilt cost $2.25, how much did the whole quilt cost?

Name:

Work Space:

Answer:

$_____

Daily Word Problems

Friday-Week 32

Quilts

The Happy Quilters Club is having a show to display the quilts made by club members this year. Use the clues below to determine the quilt made by each quilter.

	5-Star	Flower	Crazy Quilt	Circle in Circles	Red, White, & Blue	Swirly
Rodney						
Nicole						
Sarah						
Lena						
Fred						
Marta						

1. A woman did not make the Crazy Quilt.

2. Marta patterned her quilt after bouquets from her garden.

3. Fred's interest in astronomy influenced his design.

4. Nicole's quilt used patriotic colors.

5. Sarah used a compass to make sure her shapes were accurate.

Reminder: When you know that a quilt was **not** made by someone, make an X under that quilt and across from that person's name. When you know that quilt **was** made by a person, write YES in that box. You can then X that quilt for all the other names **and** X all the other quilts for that person.

Daily Word Problems

Monday-Week 33

Mail Center

To mail a small package at the Mail Center, it costs 54¢ for the first ounce and 43¢ for each additional ounce. How much more would it cost to mail seven 1-ounce packages than to mail one package weighing 7 ounces?

Name:

Work Space:

Answer:

_____¢ more

Daily Word Problems

Tuesday-Week 33

Mail Center

The Mail Center offers next-day delivery service that costs $11.75 for letters weighing 8 ounces or less. How much would it cost to mail 6 letters, if each letter weighs 8 ounces?

Name:

Work Space:

Answer:

$_____

Daily Word Problems

Wednesday-Week 33

Mail Center

The rates for 3-day delivery service are $3.20 for mail up to 2 pounds, $4.30 for mail up to 3 pounds, $5.40 for mail up to 4 pounds, and so on. How much would one 10-pound package cost?

Name:

Work Space:

Answer:

$_____

Daily Word Problems

Thursday-Week 33

Mail Center

The rates for 7-day delivery service are $2.15 for the first pound and 44¢ for each additional pound. How much would it cost to mail two 5-pound packages?

Name:

Work Space:

Answer:

$_____

Daily Word Problems • EMC 3004

Daily Word Problems

Name:

Mail Center

First-class stamp rates have increased in price over the years.

Date of Rate Change	Cost
1919	2¢
1932	3¢
1958	4¢
1963	5¢
1968	6¢
1971	8¢
1974	10¢
1975	13¢
1978	15¢
March 22, 1981	18¢
November 1, 1981	20¢
1985	22¢
1988	25¢
1991	29¢
1995	32¢
1999	33¢
2001	34¢

Use the chart to answer the following questions.

• In what year did the price go up twice?

_____

• What is the difference in price between 1919 and 2001?

_____

• In what years did the price of stamps go up more than 2 cents?

_____

Daily Word Problems

Monday-Week 34

Movies

Janet and 2 of her friends went to see a movie. The ticket prices were $4.00 each for the 3 friends and $6.50 for adults. How much did Janet and her friends pay in all? How much less did their tickets cost than 3 adult tickets?

Name:

Work Space:

Answer:

$_____ in all

$_____ less than adult tickets

Daily Word Problems

Tuesday-Week 34

Movies

Janet and her 2 friends each bought a large drink and a small bag of popcorn at the concession stand. Large drinks cost $3.25 each and small bags of popcorn cost $3.50 each. How much did each person spend? How much did they spend in all?

Name:

Work Space:

Answer:

$_____ each

$_____ in all

Daily Word Problems

Wednesday-Week 34

Movies

Janet wanted to tell her mother what time to pick her up after the movie. The movie starts at 2:20 p.m. and runs for 1 hour and 47 minutes. What time should Janet tell her mother to pick her up?

Name:

Work Space:

Answer:

_____ : _____ p.m.

Daily Word Problems

Thursday-Week 34

Movies

Janet wanted to know how many people were watching the movie in the theater. There were 30 rows with 20 seats in each row. Janet noticed that 60 seats were empty. How many people were watching the movie?

Name:

Work Space:

Answer:

_____ people

Daily Word Problems • EMC 3004

Daily Word Problems

Name:

Movies

The movie schedule in the newspaper got all mixed up. Use the clues below to find out which movie is playing at each theater.

	Space Clowns	Hit That Ball!	Undersea Adventure	Manny the Monster	Pets on Parade
Bizou					
Galaxy					
Super Cinema					
Giant Screen					
Big-O-Rama					

1. The movie at Big-O-Rama is out of this world.

2. Leon wants to see a sports movie so he's going to the Super Cinema.

3. The movie that has dogs, cats, and goldfish is playing at the theater that is third in alphabetical order.

4. Grab your snorkel and head for the Bizou.

Reminder: When you know that a movie is **not** at a specific theater, make an **X** under that movie and across from that theater name. When you know that a move **is** at a specific theater, write **YES** in that box. You can then X that movie for all the other theaters **and** X all the other movies for that theater.

Daily Word Problems

Monday-Week 35

Summer Camp

Each summer Ian goes to summer camp just outside Rocky Mountain National Park. Ian lives in Greeley, Colorado, which is at an elevation of 4,663 feet. The elevation at the camp is 8,023 feet. How much higher is the camp than Greeley, Colorado?

Name:

Work Space:

Answer:

_____ feet higher

Daily Word Problems

Tuesday-Week 35

Summer Camp

Ian went on a hike that started at an altitude of 8,023 feet and went through these stages:

Start	-	8,023 ft
Stage #1	-	8,092 ft
Stage #2	-	8,144 ft
Stage #3	-	8,220 ft

Help Ian find the elevation gained at each stage of the hike. Which stage had the greatest increase in elevation? Which stage had the smallest increase?

Name:

Work Space:

Answer:

_____ had greatest increase

_____ had smallest increase

Daily Word Problems

Wednesday-Week 35

Summer Camp

The 3-legged race is one of the field day activities at the camp. Twenty campers participate in the race at a time. There are 200 campers. How many individual races need to take place for everyone to have a chance to race? If each race takes 5 minutes, how long will it take for everyone to race?

Name:

Work Space:

Answer:

_____ individual races

_____ minutes for all races

Daily Word Problems

Thursday-Week 35

Summer Camp

Ian is passing out marshmallows for a marshmallow roast. There are 45 marshmallows in a bag and 200 campers. How many bags of marshmallows will Ian need so that everyone has 6 marshmallows? How many marshmallows will be left over?

Name:

Work Space:

Answer:

_____ bags

_____ left over

Daily Word Problems

Name:

Summer Camp

One of Ian's favorite activities at the camp is hiking. Here is a map of his two favorite trails.

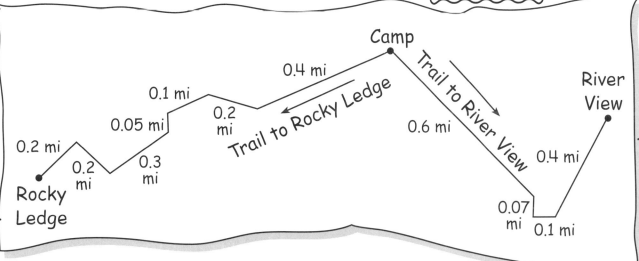

Camp

0.4 mi

0.1 mi

0.05 mi

0.2 mi

Trail to Rocky Ledge

0.2 mi

0.2 mi

0.3 mi

Rocky Ledge

Trail to River View

0.6 mi

River View

0.4 mi

0.07 mi

0.1 mi

• How long is the trail to Rocky Ledge?

_____

• How long is the trail to River View?

_____

• Which trail is longer? How much longer is it?

_____   _____

Daily Word Problems

Monday-Week 36

Water

Water might weigh more than you think. One gallon of water weighs 8.33 pounds. How much do 2 gallons of water weigh? Four gallons? Eight gallons?

Name:

Work Space:

Answer:

_____ pounds for 2 gallons

_____ pounds for 4 gallons

_____ pounds for 8 gallons

Daily Word Problems

Tuesday-Week 36

Water

Toxic chemicals are released into rivers, lakes, and other surface water in the United States every year. In 1996, 179 million pounds were released. The next year, 218 million pounds were released. How many more pounds were released in 1997 than in 1996?

Name:

Work Space:

Answer:

_____ million more pounds

Daily Word Problems • EMC 3004

Daily Word Problems

Wednesday-Week 36

Water

At sea level, water boils at 212 degrees Fahrenheit. For each 550 feet above sea level, water boils at a temperature that is one degree less. For example, at 550 feet above sea level, water boils at 211 degrees. At what temperature will water boil at 5,500 feet above sea level? At 6,600 feet above sea level?

Name:

Work Space:

Answer:

_____ degrees at 5,500 feet

_____ degrees at 6,600 feet

Daily Word Problems

Thursday-Week 36

Water

The Great Lakes are a group of five large freshwater lakes in North America. Lake Superior contains 2,935 cubic miles of water, Lake Michigan contains 1,180 cubic miles, Lake Huron contains 850 cubic miles, Lake Ontario contains 393 cubic miles, and Lake Erie contains 116 cubic miles. What is the total volume of water for all the Great Lakes?

Name:

Work Space:

Answer:

_____ total cubic miles of water

Daily Word Problems

Friday-Week 36

Name:

Water

Ms. Holloway made this chart to show how much water six different students drink each day. Write a word problem that uses this data and then solve your problem.

Amount of Water Students Drink Each Day

Student	Number of Glasses of Water	Number of Ounces in Each Glass
A	2	8
B	3	8
C	2	12
D	3	12
E	2	16
F	3	16

_____

_____

_____

_____

_____

_____

Answer: _____

Answer Key

Week 1
Monday—72 pencils
Tuesday—24 days
Wednesday—$0.20
Thursday—$9.80
Friday—$23.00

Week 2
Monday—A seed should be drawn between $2\frac{1}{2}$ and 3 centimeters from the bottom of the jar.
Tuesday—$12\frac{1}{2}$ centiliters
Wednesday—4 days; 7 days; 3 days longer
Thursday—49 millimeters longer
Friday—Seed C; Seeds A, B, and F; Seed A

Week 3
Monday—15 classrooms
Tuesday—3 members did not vote
Wednesday—158 students voted for Toby; Gail won
Thursday—$350.00 collected; $175.00 profit
Friday—The complete basketball set is the better deal; It costs $5 more to buy the items separately.

Week 4
Monday—7 packs
Tuesday—$27.00
Wednesday—102 spikes; $51.00
Thursday—30 alyssum, 15 bells of Ireland, 15 calendula
Friday—$3.75, $3.80, $2.55, $1.98, $1.05; Total $13.13

Week 5
Monday—17 milliliters
Tuesday—30 milliliters of water; 10 milliliters of cooking oil
Wednesday—32 minutes longer
Thursday—5° hotter
Friday—25 ml on Day 2, 37 ml on Day 3, 32 ml on Day 4, 41 ml on Day 5; Most on Day 5, Least on Day 1; Answers will vary, but estimates should be about 6 or 7 days and 33 to 35 ml of water was evaporating each day.

Week 6
Monday—1 minute, 36 seconds
Tuesday—2,800 meters
Wednesday—$8\frac{3}{4}$ hours in 1 week; $43\frac{3}{4}$ hours in 5 weeks
Thursday—13 minutes, 36 seconds
Friday—3 seconds faster; 5 minutes, 10 seconds; 12 seconds slower; 4 minutes, 54 seconds

Week 7
Monday—$10.50
Tuesday—8:40 p.m.
Wednesday—$4.00 per hour
Thursday—$27.00
Friday—$1,196.00; $598.00; There are many possible combinations that do not exceed $46, including the following: CD player and book; camera, video game, and book; camera, CD, and book

Week 8
Monday—84 years
Tuesday—25 light bulbs
Wednesday—18 cylinders
Thursday—200 films
Friday—1,560; 3,217; 9,480; 7,561,028

Week 9
Monday—$5.00; 12 fish
Tuesday—$56.04
Wednesday—32 babies in all; 37 angelfish in all
Thursday—$9.60 for 24; $9.20 for 23
Friday—14, 17, 20, 23, 26, 29, 44, 59, 89, 149; The rule is to multiply by 3 and then subtract 1

Week 10
Monday—1 minute, 8 seconds longer
Tuesday—6 minutes; 4 minutes
Wednesday—35 seconds; The mouse is finding the food 10 seconds faster each time.
Thursday—$10\frac{1}{2}$ gallons
Friday—Student D; Student E; 12 centimeters; fastest-0.4 seconds, slowest-0.8 seconds

Week 11
Monday—5 packages
Tuesday—8 tomatoes
Wednesday—Multiply $2 by 4; About $8.00
Thursday—4 loaves; 12 slices left over
Friday—$2.04, $20.40, $102.00; $1.92 profit

Week 12
Monday—405 jelly beans
Tuesday—2:40 p.m.
Wednesday—4 candy bars each; 12 left over
Thursday—$26.00
Friday—6, 5, 10

Week 13
Monday—10:45 a.m.
Tuesday—243 pounds
Wednesday—2 hours
Thursday—486 pounds
Friday—4 students; 15 students; 327 pounds in all

Week 14
Monday—14 ounces in 1 week; 60 ounces in 30 days
Tuesday—4 days
Wednesday—49 pancakes
Thursday—Yes, Sally had enough money because all the food together cost $5.00.
Friday—Box B-Box A is 15¢ per ounce and Box B is 12¢ per ounce; $5.25; $5.40

Week 15
Monday—408 grams
Tuesday—14 inches
Wednesday—18 cm higher
Thursday—1 m, 75 cm difference
Friday—notebook paper; 0.88 seconds; notebook paper, sandpaper, and cotton cloth; About 10 seconds

Week 16
Monday—20 feet
Tuesday—5 feet, 6 inches by 3 feet, 6 inches
Wednesday—Yes, the pictures will fit.
Thursday—38½ inches
Friday—3 feet by 4 feet; 14 feet

Week 17
Monday—8,715 feet
Tuesday—7½ hours
Wednesday—31,996 feet
Thursday—3 bottles
Friday—foothills, subalpine, foothills, montane, montane, alpine, subalpine, montane, foothills

Week 18
Monday—$168.00
Tuesday—$256.00 profit
Wednesday—3 dozen eggs; 9 dozen eggs; 30 dozen eggs
Thursday—6 days; 3 days
Friday—Edward-carrots, Lisa-beans, Ben-tomatoes, Lara-lettuce

Week 19
Monday—19.3 degrees cooler
Tuesday—856,480 miles larger
Wednesday—2,913 million miles
Thursday—About 107 times larger
Friday—Mercury, Venus, Mars. Venus-longest; Jupiter-shortest; 0.6 hours longer; 242 days longer

Week 20
Monday—613,999 square miles larger
Tuesday—7,891,957 people
Wednesday—About 350,000 people
Thursday—Fort Wayne, Indiana; Fort Wayne's population increased by 40,833 and Montgomery's population increased by 21,618
Friday—1950-1960 352,000; 1960-1970 480,000; 1970-1980 831,000; 1980-1990 781,000; Smallest-1950 to 1960; Largest-1970 to 1980; About 3,800,000 for year 2000; About 4,600,000 for year 2010

Week 21
Monday—60½ stories tall
Tuesday—1,989 megawatts
Wednesday—6,600,000
Thursday—210,000 people
Friday—1,255,000 acre-feet; 8,955,000; 9,755,000; 12,855,000; 18,693,000; 22,446,000

Week 22
Monday—$4.00 for 10 minutes; 40¢/min. compared to 43¢/min. for 5 min. and 45¢/min. for 15 min.
Tuesday—9 miles each; 36 miles in all
Wednesday—8 games each
Thursday—Bob-262 points; Carl-1,048 points; Darren-786 points
Friday—800 total points; kite

Week 23
Monday—$75 million more
Tuesday—666.6 million in 1994; 999.9 million in 1999
Wednesday—221.1 million cassettes in 1996; 147.4 million cassettes in 1998
Thursday—About 2,280 country music stations
Friday—$120.75, $89.25, $52.50, $84.00; Total 66 CDs; $346.50 profit

Week 24
Monday—128 layers
Tuesday—1994-6.8; 1995-6.9; 1906-7.7; 1985-8.1; 1923-8.3
Wednesday—About 3 miles; Round 15,400 and 5,280 to the nearest thousand and divide 15,000 by 5,000
Thursday—22.02 inches
Friday—4; 1; Devastating

Week 25
Monday—75 cigar sharks
Tuesday—208 teeth
Wednesday—10 miles; 2 hours, 15 minutes
Thursday—$48.75
Friday—mako, 1,055 more pounds; thresher, 707 more pounds; porbeagle, 447 more pounds; blue, 394 more pounds; About 19 fourth-graders; 13; 8; 8

Week 26
Monday—7.6 meters more than Opie, 4.1 meters more than Cam, 2.7 meters more than Adam, and 6.2 meters more than Bo
Tuesday—48.6 pounds
Wednesday—Opie-15 cards, Adam-45, Dana-30, Bo-60, Cam-105
Thursday—Yes, they have $31 in all and they need $30 for 5 tickets.
Friday—From top left clockwise: Hector, Frank, Morgan, Tiffany, Ahmed, Maria, Felicia

Week 27
Monday—70 millimeters
Tuesday—31 more
Wednesday—112 worms after 4 weeks; 1,792 worms after 8 weeks
Thursday—21,000 eggs in 7 sacs; 36,000 eggs in 12 sacs
Friday—80 beats/min.; 100 beats/min.; between minutes 6 and 7; minutes 9 and 10

Week 28
Monday—88 degrees warmer
Tuesday—2¼ inches
Wednesday—73 years
Thursday—36 degrees
Friday—40 minutes; 50 minutes; 1 hour, 40 minutes; 2 hours, 5 minutes; 3 hours, 20 minutes

Week 29
Monday—209 mph faster
Tuesday—107 mph
Wednesday—21.5 miles difference
Thursday—4:30 p.m.
Friday—Amarillo, Texas; Miami, Florida; 1,705 miles; 1,277 miles